Helping hands

It was a spring morning.
The kids were helping Mum
and Dad with lots of jobs.
Nat was helping Mum in
the garden.

The flowers were in bloom
and so were the weeds.

Nat pulled a bunch of weeds and filled a bucket. Mum looked into her bucket.

Dan had pulled the sheets off his bed. He loaded them in and added Nat's bright green top.

Then he tipped some
liquid in and turned it on.

Dad had a broom and was sweeping. Sam had a bucket and a mop and was sploshing suds here and there.

Dad said, "Perhaps a little less liquid, Sam. We might slip in all that wet."
Dad put some towels down.

Dan's load finished. He grabbed the sheets and Nat's top and went out to hang them up with pegs.

Mum looked at the sheets and said, "Green sheets! That's interesting."

Nat started to scrub the shower.
"That's shampoo!" said Dad.
"It might be better
for our hair."

Dan tipped the milk down
the sink.
"Yuck! This old milk
is off!" he said.
Mum said, "That's
custard, dear."

Nat was dusting and a brown dish fell off the shelf. Smash! "It's just a little crack," she said.

Sam picked up the mat and shook it hard to get the muck off. Dust flicked on Mum and Dad.

Mum and Dad said, "Thanks kids, you have been a big help. But we will do the rest!"

Words to blend

spring	helping	bunch
help	sploshing	grabbed
interesting	scrub	custard
milk	dusting	shelf
smash	just	crack
flicked	rest	shook
shower	bucket	liquid

Before reading

Synopsis: The kids are helping Mum and Dad with the tasks. They try to do their best, but will they succeed?

Review graphemes/phonemes: ow oo igh ee ar

Story discussion: Look at the cover and read the title together. Ask: *Who is helping in the picture? What are they doing? Do you ever help with the chores at home? What kinds of things do you do?*

Link to prior learning: Display a word with adjacent consonants from the story, e.g. *bright*. Ask the children to put a dot under the single-letter graphemes (*b, r, t*) and a line under the trigraph (*igh*). Model, if necessary, how to sound out and blend the sounds together to read the word. Repeat with another word from the story, e.g. *sweeping*, and encourage children to sound out and blend the word independently.

Vocabulary check: suds – soapy foam

Decoding practice: Display the word *grabbed*. Focus on the *ed* at the end, and remind children that in some words, these two letters make a /d/ sound at the end of the word. Sound out and blend all through the word: g-r-a-bb-d.

Tricky word practice: Display the word *little* and ask children to point out the tricky part of the word (*le*, which makes the /l/ sound). Practise writing and reading the word.

After reading

Apply learning: Ask: *Why did Mum and Dad decide to do the housework by themselves at the end?* (The children had accidentally got things wrong and caused a few problems.)

Comprehension

- Who does the gardening?

- Who mops the floor?

- What happens when Dan washes Nat's top with the sheets?

Fluency

- Pick a page that most of the group read quite easily. Ask them to reread it with pace and expression. Model how to do this if necessary.

- Ask children to turn to page 13 and read the conversation between Dan and Mum with lots of expression.

- Practise reading the words on page 17.

Tricky words review

was	were	so
pulled	said	oh
they	he	some
little	put	be
she	old	do